Edited by
ANDREW ROBERTS
NEIL JOHNSON
and **TOM MILTON**

PRAYER

❝ They devoted themselves
to the apostles' teaching and to
fellowship, to the breaking
of bread and **to prayer.** **❞**

The Bible Reading Fellowship
15 The Chambers, Vineyard
Abingdon OX14 3FE
brf.org.uk

The Bible Reading Fellowship (BRF) is a Registered Charity (233280)

ISBN 978 0 85746 681 5
First published 2018
10 9 8 7 6 5 4 3 2 1 0
All rights reserved

Acknowledgements
Unless otherwise acknowledged, scripture quotations from The New Revised Standard Version of the Bible, Anglicised edition, copyright © 1989, 1995 by the Division of Christian Education of the National Council of the churches of Christ in the United States of America. Used by permission. All rights reserved.

Scripture quotations on cover and title page, or marked NIV, are taken from The Holy Bible, New International Version (Anglicised edition) copyright © 1979, 1984, 2011 by Biblica. Used by permission of Hodder & Stoughton Publishers, a Hachette UK company. All rights reserved. 'NIV' is a registered trademark of Biblica. UK trademark number 1448790.

Scripture quotations taken from the Holy Bible, New Living Translation, copyright © 1996, 2004, 2007, 2013. Used by permission of Tyndale House Publishers, Inc., Carol Stream, Illinois 60188. All rights reserved.

Photographs on pages 4 and 24 copyright © Thinkstock; photographs on pages 14, 23, 28, 35, 43, 52 and 63 copyright © Tom Milton and the Birmingham Methodist Circuit.

Every effort has been made to trace and contact copyright owners for material used in this resource. We apologise for any inadvertent omissions or errors, and would ask those concerned to contact us so that full acknowledgement can be made in the future.

A catalogue record for this book is available from the British Library

Printed and bound by CPI Group (UK) Ltd, Croydon CR0 4YY

CONTENTS

To order more copies of the Holy Habits resources, or to find out how to download pages for printing or projection on screen, please visit brfonline.org.uk/holy-habits.

Remember the context

This Holy Habit is set in the context of ten Holy Habits, and the ongoing life of your church and community.

> **They devoted themselves to** the apostles' teaching and fellowship, to the breaking of bread and the **prayers**. Awe came upon everyone, because many wonders and signs were being done by the apostles. All who believed were together and had all things in common; they would sell their possessions and goods and distribute the proceeds to all, as any had need. Day by day, as they spent much time together in the temple, they broke bread at home and ate their food with glad and generous hearts, praising God and having the goodwill of all the people. And day by day the Lord added to their number those who were being saved.
>
> ACTS 2:42–47

A prayer for the faithful practice of Holy Habits

This prayer starts with a passage from Romans 5:4–5.

> Endurance produces character, and character produces hope,
>   and hope does not disappoint us…
> Gracious and ever-loving God, we offer our lives to you.
> Help us always to be open to your Spirit in our thoughts
>   and feelings and actions.
> Support us as we seek to learn more about those habits of the Christian life
>   which, as we practise them, will form in us the character of Jesus
>   by establishing us in the way of faith, hope and love.
> Amen

INTRODUCTION

Prayer is a foundational and transformative Holy Habit, a way of being, the breath of life. It reorientates us in right relationships with God, with others and the world. It is an antidote to the selfishness of sin.

There are many helpful ways of thinking about **Prayer**. One is by using the letters of ACTS:

Adoration: When did you last spend time: expressing your adoration of God just for the sake of it? Reorienting yourself in the orbit of God's love? Gazing upon and being transformed by divine holiness?

Confession: This can sometimes be rushed. It is tempting to focus on the repentance (the changing and moving on) without first dwelling in the place of contrition and sorrow.

Thanksgiving: Another transformational aspect of **Prayer**, which fosters humility as well as **Gladness and Generosity**. The simple practice of saying grace before a meal connects us with the goodness of God in creation, while the great thanksgiving prayers from many Communion services remind us of how much we have to be grateful for, most especially in the self-giving love of God seen in the life, death and resurrection of Jesus.

Supplication: As we take time with adoration, confession and thanksgiving, we are reorientated to God's love and holiness. So, when we come to supplication (or intercession), we are able to pray in a way consistent with the teaching of Jesus for the fruits of God's kingdom to be seen and known in the lives of those for whom we pray.

There are two great biblical cries of **Prayer**: the cry of praise typified by the word 'Hallelujah', and the cry of lament captured in phrases such as 'How long?' God is shown to hear and respond to both cries. Be sure to explore this habit from both these perspectives, confident in the one to whom you pray, who holds and hears you as you do.

Reflections

Whenever Christians meet together, they pray. Sometimes the words are well loved and have been recited by the church for ages past. Sometimes the words are fresh and raw, gushing from the deep cries of people's hearts. On other occasions, **Prayer** is silent. Or **Prayer** may arise simply from the shared activity of people who love Jesus Christ 'living, working in our world'.

Prayer is a conversation with God; it is waiting on God – both in listening and serving. **Prayer** is sustaining, encouraging, nurturing, exciting and engaging. It is the lifeblood of the church.

As you explore the Holy Habit of **Prayer**, we hope churches will be encouraged to pray together, not just in corporate worship but perhaps in prayer meetings or small groups.

- How could the **Prayer** life of individuals be strengthened and developed?
- Could **Prayer** be used as a tool for mission?
- How/where else could **Prayer** be or become a regular feature of your church life?

And in the community of which you are a part:

- What does **Prayer** mean to people who are not in the church?
- How can the church be part of the community through its **Prayer**?
- Where is **Prayer** happening already in your local community, and how can you engage with that?

And when we are struggling to pray, or when prayers are not answered in the way we hope or expect, how can we support one another to wrestle with that before God in **Prayer**?

 Resources particularly suitable for children and families
☺ Resources particularly suitable for young people

CH4 Church Hymnary 4 (also known as Hymns of Glory Songs of Praise)
RS Rejoice and Sing
SoF Songs of Fellowship 6
StF Singing the Faith

UNDERSTANDING THE HABIT

WORSHIP RESOURCES

Below are some thoughts and ideas for how you might incorporate this Holy Habit into worship.

Biblical material

Old Testament passages:

- Exodus 2 onwards — The story of Moses, who spoke to God 'as one speaks to a friend'
- Job 30:20–31 — Job speaks of his anguish
- Psalm 43 — A psalm of lament
- Psalm 139 — O God, you search me and you know me
- Jeremiah 29:4–7 — Pray for the welfare of the place to which I have sent you

Gospel passages:

- Matthew 6:5–15 — The Lord's Prayer
- Matthew 7:7 — Ask and you will receive
- Mark 1:29–38 — Jesus heals and prays
- Mark 11:24–25 — Whatever you ask in prayer
- Luke 11:1–13 — The Lord's Prayer
- Luke 22:39–46 — Jesus prays on the Mount of Olives

Other New Testament passages:

- Acts 13:1–3 — Prayer and fasting
- Romans 8:26–27 — The Spirit and prayer
- Philippians 4:4–9 — Rejoice in the Lord always
- Colossians 3:12–17, 23–24 — Whatever you do, do it wholeheartedly
- Colossians 4:2–4 — Be steadfast in prayer
- 1 Thessalonians 5:16–18 — Never stop praying

Suggested hymns and songs

When we think about **Prayer**, it is tempting to think that our prayers must always be spoken aloud, but of course there are many ways of praying. The hymns and songs suggested for this Holy Habit are sometimes about **Prayer**, but they are mostly hymns and songs that we can use instead of spoken prayers as individuals or in corporate worship. Some of them are words of scripture about **Prayer** and some can be used when we cannot find the words to pray for ourselves.

- Because you came and sat beside us (StF 420)
- Create in me (SoF 2760) ☺
- Faithful One, so unchanging (StF 628)
- For the healing of the nations (CH4 706, RS 620, StF 696)
- Hear me, dear Lord, in this my time of sorrow (CH4 729)
- How long, O Lord, will you forget (StF 630)
- Hungry (SoF 1293) ☺
- I am (SoF 3079) ☺
- Jesus, remember me (CH4 775, StF 777)
- Lord you sometimes speak in wonders (CH4 606, StF 158)
- Lord, I need you (Sof 2422) ☺
- Lord, in our lonely hours (StF 616)
- Make me a channel of your peace (CH4 528, RS 629, StF 707) 🧑‍🤝‍🧑
- O Lord, hear our prayer (RS 398)
- Prayer is like a telephone (KS 286) 🧑‍🤝‍🧑
- Thank you, O God, for the time that is now (StF 478)
- The Lord's Prayer (StF 762 or 763)
- There's nothing worth more (Holy Spirit) (SoF 3020) ☺
- This we can do for justice and peace (RS 639)
- We pray for peace (RS 641, StF 719)
- When I'm feeling down and sad (CH4 568, StF 642)
- When, O God, our faith is tested (StF 643)
- You are before me, Lord, you are behind (CH4 96, RS 731)

For further suggestions, see StF 517–531 (Prayer: Intercession and Petition), or search Singing the Faith Plus (**www.singingthefaithplus.org.uk**).

Introduction to the theme 👨‍👩‍👧

Start with some general questions to the congregation:

- How do you pray?
- Where do you pray?
- Do you do anything special with your hands or eyes?
- What words do you use?
- Does it matter what sort of things we pray about?

Then tell this story from 1 Samuel 1:

> There's a story in the Bible about a woman called Hannah. She was very sad because she didn't have any children. She was upset because people teased her and said it was her fault. They boasted to her about their children.
>
> One day Hannah went to the temple to pray. She was really upset and she cried as she prayed. Eli, the priest, saw her praying. He could see her lips moving but couldn't hear anything. Eli thought Hannah was drunk and so he told her off. Hannah explained how upset she was and told Eli that she was pouring her heart out to God. Then Eli understood and told her to go in peace.
>
> Hannah's prayers were answered and sometime later she had a baby. Things don't always turn out the way we want them to when we pray to God. But Hannah knew that she could say anything to God and God would listen.

It doesn't matter if we're happy or sad, calm or cross; we can tell God exactly how life is and God will listen. The Psalms are full of songs and poems where people tell God exactly how they're feeling. Maybe you could try reading some of them if you don't know how to pray – you may just find one that says how it is for you.

But we also need to take time to listen to God when we pray and not do all the talking – just like we do when we're talking to our family or friends. Because sometimes when we pray God says 'Yes', and sometimes God says 'No', and sometimes God says 'Wait'; we need to listen because God knows what's best for us.

Finish by singing an appropriate hymn or song.

Thoughts for sermon preparation

Romans 8:26–27

> The Spirit comes to the aid of our weakness. We do not even know how we ought to pray, but through our inarticulate groans the Spirit himself is pleading for us, and God who searches our inmost being knows what the Spirit means.

God is the heart of the world and the heart of our own hearts, the source of all that is, the life in all life, the truth we touch in all our search for meaning. God loves us into being, and in that loving enables us to grow and to experience more deeply the sorrow and the joy of the world, and to live lives that are thankful, humble and open to wonder. **Prayer** is the breathing of that life, the struggle to find words which express both our deepest desires and our darkest insights into who we are and what we are capable of. In every situation, **Prayer** is a possibility and therefore an invitation. A moment of sheer thankfulness in the day. Watching at the bedside of a dying loved one. A cry for help when we don't know how we will be able to deal with some crisis. A bewildered love that reaches out in response to the need of people thousands of miles away. A glimpse of glory that draws wonder from the depths of us. A silence before reading the Bible or at the end of the day. All of these are praying, reaching out to God with longing. Sometimes we try to express that longing in (always inadequate) words, and Paul reminds us that, in that groping after language, the Holy Spirit is weaving a prayer in us.

However natural or difficult we may find praying on our own, something happens when we come together to pray, whether in twos or threes or in worship together as a congregation. Together we are the body of Christ, so when we pray together, we pray as Christ's body. In the language of the letter to the Hebrews, Jesus is the great High Priest, our representative in heaven. Jesus knows our weakness, our slowness and hardness of heart, and loves us anyway, and gives himself for the life of the world. We don't have to have **Prayer** all worked out. We pray in the name of Jesus, so Jesus takes our prayer into the heart of God.

This resource invites us to make **Prayer** a Holy Habit, both on our own and when we come together. May **Prayer** be the spiritual breath we breathe and may it deepen love's transforming power in the world.

Prayers

A reflection on the Lord's Prayer

Father and mother of us all, with us, yet not of this world,
your name is precious to us.

We long to see the world as you would have it,
as we know it will become,
but for now we are thankful for the things we need here today –
food, shelter, health, love and enough to do.

We know we are not always the people you would like us to be –
we fail you, ourselves and each other
and we are not as forgiving as we could be –
so we ask that we might know ourselves made new
and set free to release others from our anger and hurt.

Though life is full of temptations,
help us to stand firm
and keep us from straying down the wrong paths.

All this we ask because we know that
you are the power that keeps us loving,
yours is the kingdom we inhabit by faith
and through us we hope the world will see
the wonder that is your love and grace.

As Jesus has taught us and as the Holy spirit urges us –
so we pray.
Amen

A prayer for the day

This prayer was inspired by the poem 'Sheep Fair Day' by Kerrie Hardy, and explores the upcoming day of the writer. Invite people to use this as a model to walk through their day in **Prayer**, sharing intimate detail with God and placing the day into his hands.

Come with me today, God:

Walk with me and the dog to collect the paper – listen to birds, notice the new colours in the flower beds, greet the people we meet regularly on this road.

Listen to the radio with me over breakfast – feel the frustration with politicians who will not answer questions, laugh at the banter between presenters who have become old friends.

Sit in the car with me as I drive to a meeting – learn patience with other drivers in the rush hour, watch the speed as we go down the motorway, talk through the agenda in advance and think about the people we are going to meet.

Walk with me through the city – notice the ones who are striding and confident and the ones who shuffle, the ones who sell the *Big Issue* or are even now rolling up the sleeping bag they slept on the pavement in; agonise over whether to give or not – have we got change? Have we got the time to stop?

Sit with me and my planning group – enjoy our growing friendship and trust in each other, listen as we focus and digress by turns, share our excitement at a good event coming together.

Come home with me and collapse on the settee with the iPad, checking Facebook and emails, listening to H's day and wondering what we will eat this evening: one of the children has had a difficult time at work – feel the knot of worry at the pit of the stomach that will rest there until I speak with her myself.

Join me in doing bits of housework – hanging washing and tidying up – and if it's fine some gardening – weeding mainly, picking fruit if there is some, picking courgettes and wondering what we are going to do with them all.

Then sit down with H and the dog and some knitting to watch something on the television – feel smug when we answer the questions on *University Challenge* or *Only Connect*, work out who the murderer is, and despair once again at the state of your world.

So at the end of day, when I replay it before you, I will know that you have been there, that you are with me, loving, caring, challenging, reassuring, and I can rest in your peacefulness until the new day dawns.
Amen

A prayer of lament

O Lord, our Lord,
how hard it is to be your chosen people.

How hard to feel secure within a lifeboat
when the sea around is full of those who fight to stay afloat.

How hard to be among a team of winners
and face the sadness and dejection of those who've lost.

How hard to hear our songs of triumph
whilst in our heart we yearn for those who struggle yet.

How hard to contemplate your throne of glory
when our suffering world cries out for peace and bread.

O Lord, our Lord,
how hard it is to be your chosen people:
how hard.

A prayer in the clamour

Dear God,
this is a noisy world,
so many different voices scream for our attention:

the child is bounced by TV ads for toys
and so responds, 'I want that... and that... and that!'

the student is engulfed by credit offers;
loans, overdrafts, cards to make your life more sweet.

the retired receive seductive invitations to cash in their home
to meet the necessary costs of growing old.

How on earth, dear God, are we to hear,
within this clamouring din, your word of truth?

Tune our hearts and ears that we might know
and, knowing, live your wise and holy way.

A prayer asking for forgiveness

Forgive us, Father God,
if, when confronted by
deep human need,
our knees weaken
and resolve fades.

Forgive our fear of failure
when we take the risk
of acting confidently in faith.

Inspire us with stories
where faith and action intertwine.
And, as we falteringly
follow where you lead,
raise our expectations of
your power at work in human life.

Raise our hope that
your kingdom is much more
than wishful words.
Raise up, through us, the fallen ones
you place within our care.
Amen

A prayer of thanksgiving

When our souls are parched
and we cry out for moisture

You are present even in our dryness

When strong forces are set to undermine
the way of love and life we have from you

You are present even in our weakness

When memories of joyful, easy times recede
and uncertainty stalks our future days

Your presence is our purpose and our peace

When we think all hope is gone
then notice that still your light burns clear and strong

**Faithful God,
our hope,
our truth,
our joy,
We praise you!**

A prayer of intercession

Introduction to intercessory prayers.

Lord, in our weakness we come to you for strength,
In our sorrow we come to you for comfort,
In our joy we come to you to celebrate with us,
In our times of anxiety we come to you for succour,
In times of confusion and doubt we come to you for guidance and help,
So now we come to pray for ourselves and others.

In Jesus' name
Amen

A prayer of thanksgiving

Based on 1 Thessalonians 5:16–18.

We give thanks for all you have given us.
We come before you with grateful, thankful hearts,
giving thanks whatever our circumstances.
We pray without ceasing and
praise you for the abundance you have placed in our hands.
May our prayers be ever thankful and our hearts full of joy,
As we praise and thank you for the abundance of your creation.
We give thanks for all you have given us.
We come before you with grateful, thankful hearts,
giving thanks whatever our circumstances.
We pray without ceasing and
praise you for the abundance you have placed in our hands.

May our prayers be ever thankful and our hearts full of joy,
As we praise and thank you for the abundance of your creation.
May we rejoice and give thanks, for you
have placed every good thing under our hand, you are Lord.
You welcome us into a relationship with you,
you delight in our prayers,
you know the thoughts of our hearts and minds,
yet welcome our conversation through prayer.
Thank you, Lord, for who you are,
thank you for your redeeming love and grace to us.
Thank you for the gift of your Son,
that through his death and resurrection we have been reconciled with you.
Amen

A prayer for peace

Lead me from death to life, from falsehood to truth.
Lead me from despair to hope, from fear to trust.
Lead me from hate to love, from war to peace.
Let peace fill our hearts, our world, our universe.
Amen

Different ways of praying

The Lord's Prayer

Explain that it can be easy to say the Lord's Prayer without thinking, because it is so familiar.

Put the words of the Lord's Prayer on the screen or find it in a hymn book or service book and ask the congregation to read through the words slowly, taking time to savour each word and phrase. Give them at least five minutes.

Then say it slowly together.

You may also choose to pray the Lord's Prayer in a variety of other ways, such as singing, or using art or bodily movement.

Sung prayers

Choose hymns or songs to replace spoken prayers. If you like the words but don't know the tune, they could be read aloud together.

Many hymn books have an index which helps you find appropriate prayers.

Or try using a verse or chorus interspersed between spoken prayers.

'Liturgical settings' in *Singing the Faith* or other hymn books could be particularly helpful for this.

A prayer for when there are no words

Find a comfortable position and choose a word or two to breathe in and out slowly as you become more aware of God's presence and relax into it. For example:

Yahweh
Abba
Jesus
Amen
Love me

A prayer following a tragedy

We have come together in this place, our God, because there is nowhere else to go with such grief, such shock, such anger.

We have not got the words we need to pray, for words need clarity and we are not at all certain how we feel with so many emotions racing through us.
Lord, have mercy

Play or have someone sing a Kyrie and invite people to let the music wash over them as the love of God. Give permission to sit or kneel, hold each other or sit apart.

Give space for those who would like to offer prayer out loud. When the time is right:

Christ, have mercy and help us to hear again the confident words of Paul spoken to us now:

'For I am convinced that neither death, nor life, nor angels, nor rulers, nor things present, nor things to come, nor powers, nor height, nor depth, nor anything else in all creation, will be able to separate us from the love of God in Christ Jesus our Lord' (Romans 8:38–39).

Offer the opportunity to light a candle, or write a name to hang on a branch, or perform some similar action, while music is playing again.

Lord, have mercy on us as we go from this place. Go with us and hold us as we support each other until we are ready to face the world again.

Bless us and keep us in your love.
Amen

Silent prayer

Perhaps use silence or quiet music to encourage the congregation to listen for God. It can be difficult to hold our prayerful intentions in silence even for a couple of minutes. In order to help people in this, reflect again on the section earlier in this booklet: 'A prayer for when there are no words'. The use of one or two prayerful words can be a way to gently bring ourselves back to worshipful silence before God when our thoughts wander.

Thomas Keating, in his books on Centering Prayer (e.g. *Open Mind, Open Heart,* Continuum, 2006), says that it is important not to think that this use of a prayer-word is like using a mantra, nor is the word to be repeated mechanically – it is an expression of loving intention towards God.

Silent prayer is intended to make words such as those of Isaiah 30:15 – 'In quietness and in trust shall be your strength' – real in our lives, but it is wise to start small, whether in personal or congregational prayer, with just two minutes of silence, perhaps at first simply as a way of preparing people for a time of vocal prayer.

Prayers using all the senses

You may find it helpful to explore how to use all of your senses in prayer. Think about how you could use your sense of touch by holding or feeling items when praying. Could you use your sense of taste or smell, for example using food?

Praying in other languages

Provide opportunities for people to pray and lead prayer in other languages, as a way of celebrating diversity within the body of Christ and affirming the gifts and graces of those for whom English is not their first language.

Remember and encourage the use of sign language or Makaton.

Where children are learning new languages, encourage them to offer prayers in the languages they are learning.

Praying the Lord's Prayer simultaneously in various languages can be a powerful and moving experience.

Twister prayers 👪 ☺

Either use the spinner from the game Twister or create a similar colour dial.

Spin the dial and use the colours as a prompt for prayers. This could be done in a variety of ways:

- Each colour might be used for a type of prayer (e.g. if the spinner stops on blue – adoration, yellow – confession, etc.)
- More specific prayer topics might be written on coloured card matching the colours on the dial, but retaining the connection between a colour and a type of prayer.
- The different colours might be used to prompt prayers of intercession under different headings (blue – church, yellow – local community, etc.). Again, coloured cards might be used to provide for specific prayers.
- More creatively, each colour might be linked to praying in a particular way rather than to a particular type of prayer: using words; using silence; thinking of (or playing/singing) a piece of music, song or hymn; thinking of (or drawing/sketching) an image or picture.

Washing-line prayers 👪 ☺

Washing-line prayers can be used in a variety of ways – all you need is a long piece of string (or washing line), some pegs and something to write on. Invite people to draw or write something they want to thank God for and then peg their prayer to the washing line. Alternatively, peg newspaper headlines to the washing line as a prayer of intercession.

Prayer wristbands ☺

Prayer wristbands can be used in many ways and are helpful in forming the habit of **Prayer** as the wristband is worn and is a constant reminder to pray.

For example, put different coloured beads in different bowls with some string. Write out Colossians 1:3, 9–12 on a large card.

Read the verses together and then point out how Paul always thanked God for the faithful people at Colossae and never stopped praying for them.

Choose a bead for each person that you want to pray for. Put the beads on the string and let it help you to remember to pray for those people each day.

GROUP MATERIAL AND ACTIVITIES

Some of these small group materials are traditional Bible studies, some are more diverse session plans and others are short activities, reflections and discussions. Please choose materials appropriate to whatever group you are working with.

Creative acts of worship 👨‍👩‍👧 ☺

Think about alternative ways to structure your acts of worship, which can provide an opportunity to find new ways of expressing yourselves in **Prayer**. For some churches, to be active in acts of worship can helps spiritual truths sink in more easily than many words. For others, creativity might mean exploring liturgy or ancient practices.

Praying with the psalms of lament

Psalm 43

> In prayer, all is not sweetness and light. The way of prayer is not to cover our unlovely emotions so that they will appear respectable, but expose them so that they can be enlisted in the work of the kingdom.
>
> Eugene Peterson

The Psalms are a wonderful aid in **Prayer**, and give us language and words to speak to God in whatever state we find ourselves – whether in joy or grief, celebration or suffering. The Psalms formed the prayer book for Israel, as well as for Jesus and the early Christians. The monastic practice of praying through the Psalms each month reflects the central role they play in Christian spirituality.

While the book of Psalms includes a number of different types of poetry – including the psalm of praise and the psalm of trust – one form of psalm perhaps less widely used in **Prayer** today is the psalm of lament.

'Psalms of lament' refers to that cluster of psalms that focus on suffering and brokenness. Such psalms give voice to the pain of the human condition, the pain of loneliness, sickness, or abandonment – even abandonment by God. Often in our spiritual life or in church, we fear to express our pain and distress at the way things are – but the psalms of lament give us words to do so.

The psalms of lament follow a fairly conventional structure, and include features such as a complaint, a petition for help and an assurance of being heard, and usually end with an expression of trust in God. Some psalms also include curses on enemies.

Other examples of psalms of lament include Psalms 12, 17, 22, 42, and 88.

There are a number of ways to pray such psalms:

Personalising the psalm
You might 'personalise' the psalm in **Prayer**, using your own words to express the emotions it expresses. This could involve writing your own paraphrase of the psalm or a prayer based upon it.

Responding to the psalm
Read each line of the psalm and allow it to prompt your own prayers of response. Psalms of lament might encourage prayers of pain, confession, or petition for God's help.

Praying for others
Psalms of lament don't always seem that relevant to our situation, particularly if life is going well. At such times, it can be helpful to allow the words of the psalm to shape your **Prayer** for others. The psalms of lament give voice to those who are in situations of suffering or despair, and allow you to bring their needs before God in **Prayer**.

For further reading on this subject, you may want to explore:

- Walter Brueggemann, *Spirituality of the Psalms* (Fortress Press, 2002)
- Eugene H. Peterson, *Answering God* (Marshall Pickering, 1996)
- Tom Wright, *Finding God in the Psalms: Sing, pray, live* (SPCK, 2014).

Jesus prays on the Mount of Olives

Luke 22:39–46

There are many different forms of **Prayer**. At the heart of all forms is an understanding of, and connection with, the character of God. Even in the places of deepest angst and lament (Job and many of the Psalms for example), there is both a reaching out to and an honouring of the faithfulness of God, that faithfulness being a rock both to rail against and to be supported by.

The ancient prayers of scripture remind us that God is big enough for all we have to throw at him and loving enough to invite our endless participation with him. They are also filled with reflections on what it is to be human. They don't tell God what to do, but they do offer us a glimpse of people allowing themselves to be fully open before God, brutally honest before God, no holds barred before God; even when such openness is to question the very existence of the one in whom the language of **Prayer** is intelligible. And all the time God not only is the creator and sustainer of all things, but is relentlessly being open to all that has been created.

There is a risk that our prayers can at times become self-absorbed (like noisy gongs; see 1 Corinthians 13:1). The purpose of this Bible study is to aid us in recovering a deeper appreciation of **Prayer** and to help us relocate our lives, however messy, confused and conflicted they might be, in God's story of love. The study focuses on a deeply personal prayer of supplication.

Read Luke 22:39–46.

You might like to explore these questions as a group, or first give time and space for people to reflect personally on them before sharing in a conversation. If weather and the time of year permit, you might like to encourage people to reflect on the text in a garden or outdoor setting. When you share together take time, allowing all those who want to share their reflections on each question. Some of your group's deepest insights will come from those who are most reluctant to share.

- What does Jesus' prayer to his Father teach me/us about the nature of God?
- Jesus firstly asks the Father to take the cup from him, and then, a little while later, submits himself fully to his Father's work in the world. How might that example influence your pattern of **Prayer**?
- Does the depth of this prayer and the context in which it is set have anything to say about our praying for minor matters? For example, should I pray for a car parking space when refugees are drowning in the sea?

fan the Flame

2TIM 1 v6

- Luke presents an angel coming to strengthen Jesus. How have you been strengthened when praying? How might you be an angel (a bringer of God's comfort) to someone praying in anguish?
- Even in his time of deepest anguish, Jesus expresses concern for his disciples and urges them (twice), in echoes of the Lord's Prayer, to pray that they will not come to the time of trial. How does Jesus' approach here helpfully challenge the possibility of being self-absorbed in **Prayer**?
- As we meet, who might be in anguish and in need of our prayers?

For further application
On the Mount of Olives, Jesus was conversing with his Father. Conversation involves speaking and listening. Some of us are better at one or the other.

If you are a good talker, take 15 minutes every day for seven days just to listen to God.

If you are a listener, take a few minutes each day simply to speak your heart to God.

The Lord's Prayer 🙌 ☺

Luke 11:1–13

Aim: for people to know the Lord's Prayer and to understand how it can be used to help them to pray.

Opening activity

Ask people what they think **Prayer** is. When do they pray and why do they pray? God wants us to talk to him and we can, a bit like a best friend who is there for us all the while. God wants to listen to us and talk to us – isn't that amazing? Because we can't see and hear God, sometimes **Prayer** can seem difficult. Jesus tells us in the Bible about a special prayer we can say just as it is and also use to help us with our own prayers.

Explain that the stories of Jesus and his teachings show that there are three good reasons to pray:

- Jesus did
- Jesus said we should
- We need God's help to live the way he wants us to.

Bible reading and activity

Read Luke 11:1–13.

For older young people or adults, you may want to spend time in a discussion around **Prayer** in general, exploring such questions as:

- When is it hard to pray?
- Are prayers always answered?
- What should prayers be about?
- How does it feel when you talk to God?
- Was it easier to pray when you were younger?

If appropriate, you may like to explore the idea of a 'prayer audit', where people think about the last week and reflect upon where and how they prayed. They may like to talk about this as a group or keep it private.

The following activity could be appropriate for all ages:

Before the session, print or write out the Lord's Prayer. You need to print or write each line on different coloured paper, enough for one between two in your group (e.g. if you have a group of 16, write the first line eight times on blue paper, the second line eight times on green paper and so on). Cut up each sheet of paper and hide the strips around the room.

Ask how many of the group know this prayer by heart. Try to pair people who can recite the Lord's Prayer with those who can't. Ask people to find one of each of the different colours and stick or place them in the correct order on to a piece of paper. Encourage people who don't know the prayer to learn it and give them some incentive to recite it for you in one or two weeks' time.

If your group is large enough, work in smaller groups of two or three. Ask each group to take one or two of the lines of the Lord's Prayer and discuss what they think it means, then write it in their own words. When everybody has completed this task, share with each other, making sure that everyone has understood what the lines mean.

Follow this by asking people to write the whole of the Lord's Prayer using their own words or in shorthand. They may like to use pictures to help express the meaning of the words. These could either be displayed or taken home.

For older young people or adults, it may be appropriate to discuss whether people think that the Lord's Prayer is helpful to them, why it might be helpful to others, or whether learning it by heart is still relevant and important in today's context.

Song

Sing a hymn or song which gives praise or thanks to God. Encourage people to think of praise songs as a way of praying too.

Final prayer

You may like to encourage people to pray for each other if that is appropriate for the group.

Finish by saying the Lord's Prayer, using the alternative words groups have discussed and then the original version all together.

Small group session: unanswered prayer 👪 ☺

Job 30:20–31

Be aware that this session may raise some uncomfortable experiences for the group, so be sensitive to what is shared.

Prepare a large printout of the passage and attach it to a wall in the room. Provide a selection of art materials (e.g. coloured A3 paper, felt-tip pens, art pastels, stickers, tubs of play dough, watercolour pencils or paints, marker pens).

Ask the group if they have ever sent a text message or message via social media and not received a reply straight away. What did that feel like? Can they describe it in a word? Examples might include 'anxious', 'impatient', 'frustrated'.

Sometimes, when we communicate with people, we don't get an instant reply and that can be hard. It can be similar when we pray or talk to God.

In the Old Testament we meet a man, Job, who up until now has enjoyed good health and wealth, and is well respected by others – his life in general has been a very comfortable and easy one. In fact, in chapter 1 God says, 'He is the finest man in all the earth' (v. 8, NLT). But at the start of this book we hear that his life has taken a turn for the worse: he loses his livestock, his children are killed and his life is now in ruins. He's suffering greatly. Through the rest of the book, we hear how this affects Job as he talks to his friends about what he's going through. Read Job 30:20–31 to hear what he says.

- Ask the group: how do you think Job is feeling? Why is he feeling this way?
- Using the large printout of the passage, ask the group to underline or circle a phrase that stands out to them – that strikes them or they find interesting. Give them a few moments to think about their choice. Invite the group to share why they chose specific phrases.
- Invite the group to use the art materials to work in pairs (although if anyone wants to do this individually then that's fine) and choose an image to illustrate. Encourage them to talk through how they would like to do this and then work together to create their artwork. Allow 15 minutes for this. At the end, let everyone view each other's pieces and see if any of the pairs would like to say a few words about what they have created.

When we pray and God doesn't seem to answer, it can be very difficult. It can affect us in a range of ways and we'll respond in a range of ways too. We might struggle to understand or know where God is in the midst of what we're going through, a bit like Job did.

If you feel able, share an example from your own life when your prayers went unanswered, or invite one or two in the group to share their experiences.

- Return to the artwork everyone has created – do any of the images remind you of how this made you feel?
- Invite the group in pairs to discuss ways we might cope with our prayers going unanswered – are there helpful things we could say or do (or not say or do)? Share these suggestions with each other.

Spend some time praying at the end of the session – depending on the group, you may want to pray about the things we feel are going unanswered, or simply ask God to help us when he seems quiet and responsive. Invite the group to join in this time.

FORMING THE HABIT

The ideas presented in this section are offered to help you establish or further practise **Prayer** as a regular habit personally, as a church and in engagement with your local community and the wider world. You may want to consider using the ideas in more than one of these contexts.

In developing **Prayer** as a regular habit, you may find some of the material in the 'Understanding the habit' section helpful too.

STORIES TO SHOW THE HABIT FORMING

How could you use these formative and transformative stories to inspire others? What stories of your own could you share?

In his book *Holy Habits* (Malcolm Down Publishing, 2016), Andrew Roberts shares these stories:

> I was once travelling with a colleague along the A38. We were doing about 65mph when we were clipped by a following vehicle, spearing us into the barriers in the middle of the road, which in turn pitched us into a roll. We came to a stop upside down in the middle of the road. Miraculously, none of the following traffic hit us. We were trapped in the car. The first two people to come to our aid were two young Muslim men. They got me out of the car and mercifully I had just a few cuts and bruises. My friend, who had been driving and therefore not able to protect herself, was in a far worse state with a badly gashed head and a broken neck. When the paramedics very carefully extricated her from the car, she asked if I would pray for her. So, kneeling in the broken glass and blood, I did. And as I prayed in the name of Jesus, the two young Muslims stood respectfully by, their heads bowed. I learned a lot that day, not least about the respect those of other faiths have for us when we pray in the name of Jesus. Thankfully, my friend went on to make a full recovery.

> When I was a student in York, I served as President of the University Christian Union. One evening we met as a leadership team with the leaders of many of the churches from across the city. We met in an upper room and began to pray. As we prayed, I experienced a real Pentecost moment. The room was so full of energy, it seemed to be shaking. It was really noisy too. I opened my eyes at one point to check that the room wasn't falling apart. I suddenly felt a great warmth going through my body – as if I had drunk a big glass of red wine in one go (I hadn't, just in case you're worried). The Holy Spirit filled us in that moment in a way that I had never known before. Sometimes prayer can be like that.

The team at Great Barr Methodist Church, who have been through the Holy Habits programme, add this story:

> Exploring the Holy Habit of **Prayer** has enriched our prayer life as a church in many ways.
>
> We have a dedicated notice board for the Holy Habits programme on which we have a permanent display of prayers. This displays basic prayers like the Lord's Prayer and other inspirational prayers and poems. We have a central spot for a prayer which is changed on a regular basis to reflect the changing seasons. The congregation is encouraged to submit a favourite prayer or inspirational words to have displayed on the board.
>
> As part of our church's 150th anniversary, we are planning to produce a booklet of 75 prayers and 75 recipes, the idea being that you make the recipe and then say the prayer before you eat it (a great example of two habits working together).
>
> We held a service led by members of the congregation based entirely on the Holy Habit of **Prayer**, which seemed to be appreciated by the congregation.
>
> The prayer group who have been meeting every Thursday morning for the last five years feel that the Holy Habit of **Prayer** has made us more aware of the importance and significance of praying, not just by yourself, but as a group. We now have prayer requests not just within our church community, but from the local community and beyond. People are amazed that we will pray for them even when they don't attend any type of church.

While exploring the Holy Habit of **Prayer**, South Yardley Methodist Church hosted a prayer day:

To do this, a group met to create interactive prayer installations in four different parts of the church building, each based on one of the elements: water, wind, fire and earth. Those involved in setting up and those who came had mostly not previously engaged with interactive prayer.

One participant commented: 'I absolutely loved this experience! It was amazing to create the spaces and lovely to be in them. I had no idea what to expect from this day but I really enjoyed all the spaces, interacting with them and taking time to be quiet and still. I realise now how little I do this and how much I need to as it enables you to just be in God's presence.'

Following this, we opened up the spaces to a group with special needs accompanied by afternoon tea and crafts. From this experience, we have been thinking more creatively about how we pray and are soon to be starting a monthly time of silence called 'Peace! Be still'. We feel that slowly we are beginning to embody the Holy Habits of **Prayer** and **Eating Together**, which will enhance our **Making More Disciples** and challenge us to be more open to offering **Generosity** and **Fellowship** to others.

PRACTICES TO HELP FORM THE HABIT

Here are some suggestions for how **Prayer** can be part of a rhythm or rule of life in our personal discipleship and in and through the **Fellowship** of our churches.

Prayer has long been an integral part of the rhythms of life of individual disciples and Christian communities. There are many ways in which it can be woven into a pattern of living.

To help those who are new to **Prayer** or unsure about it, check out the Try Praying website (**www.trypraying.co.uk**). It's a website that seeks to encourage people to pray, and promotes a 'Try Praying' booklet, a 'seven-day prayer guide for those who are not religious' and a 'Try Praying' booklet for young people and children too – check out the Resources section for more.

Often (daily or weekly)

Journalling

Journalling is regularly reflecting on your experiences, thoughts and encounters with God and keeping a note of your reflections. See the Holy Habits Introductory Guide for more information.

As you try different ways to develop the habit of **Prayer** in your day-to-day life, note in your journal what you did and how you felt, and anything that was a positive experience. Are there any ways of praying that you particularly struggle with? Where do you feel closest to God? Has **Prayer** affected your relationship with God? Has it changed your behaviour and actions in any way?

Pray! 👪 ☺

Commit 15 minutes per day to pray in a particular place in your home. Or spend an hour a week engaging in a creative prayer activity, or praying in a different place each week in your community.

Arrange a rota of people to pray each day for the life and mission of the church. Or gather to pray in small groups over issues in the news and other matters of concern.

Prayer handbooks can be a helpful way of informing and nurturing regular patterns of **Prayer**. The Methodist and United Reformed Churches, for example, publish prayer handbooks annually with suggestions for daily prayers. Denominational websites and local Christian bookshops are good places to explore prayer resources for group and personal use.

There are a number of prayer apps that can be downloaded and used on a phone or tablet, providing a prayer every day. Many websites do a similar thing.

For children, you could teach them the simple prayer, 'Help me to remember, Lord, that nothing is going to happen to me today that you and I can't handle together', or another appropriate short prayer that is easily remembered.

Prayer diary 👪 ☺

Create a prayer diary for the week. Think of things to pray for on each day, for example for someone you know who is lonely or ill, for people with exams, for those having a tough time at school or work.

Have you seen any of the prayers answered, or done anything to help the people prayed for (which itself may be an answer to prayer)?

Get into the habit of making a prayer diary for each week. You may find it helpful to have a blank template which can be filled in each week. You could do this at home or as part of a youth or children's group, church meeting or service.

Prayer map

As a church, or individually, use a large wall map of the world and flags to remind you to pray for people and situations around the world. Use a local map to pray for the local community.

Who's who?

Build a photo gallery or album of people to pray for – friends, family, members of your church, politicians and leaders.

Or why not make a list of your friends from the previous year's Christmas cards and share them out across the year, so that you pray for each one at least once during the year?

Make space in your day

Some people like to have a special place for **Prayer** which is holy, set apart. This could be as simple as a special chair, or you might find it helpful to have a cross, some things of beauty such as flowers, an icon or a picture, or a candle which can be lit as you pray.

Could you use a public place such as a local park or a street corner as your special place? Sit on a bench, spend some time watching the people going by and pray for them. If you are in the countryside or a place of beauty, stop, observe and give thanks.

Could you make this a regular practice? Part of your daily commute, the school run, the dog walk?

Pray your day

Each day, with your diary open, pray through your day. If you pray at the beginning of the day, pray about how you might be challenged that day. If you pray at the end of the day, pray about how your day has affected you. Which people, meetings and events do you specially need to pray for?

Sometimes (weekly or monthly)

Pray with others 👨‍👩‍👦 ☺

It is often easier to share and explore **Prayer** with others. Form prayer pairs, prayer triplets or prayer groups and meet up regularly to pray (or use internet messaging or video calling tools to meet virtually). Be open, welcoming, supportive and encouraging of one another.

Remember to consider age, gender and safeguarding when putting prayer groups of any size together.

Many churches have a prayer chain – members all know how to contact the next person in the chain so that, whoever receives the prayer request, it can get passed around the chain and all can pray.

Endeavour to keep **Prayer** fresh by:

- encouraging different people to lead in **Prayer**
- exploring different ways of praying, including silent prayer, body prayers and prayer that uses art and symbols
- ensuring there is a balanced diet of **Prayer** (praise and lament – adoration, confession, thanksgiving and supplication)
- using different resources and traditions of **Prayer**

As part of your mutual accountability, have one meeting a year in which you review your prayer life, both personally and as a group.

Could you keep a prayer book in your youth group or meeting or for use in your church services? Record prayer requests from people and pray for them whenever the group meets, or as part of your services. Every so often, you can look back through the book and reflect upon whether and how these prayers have been answered – or recall those that haven't. This could help a group or congregation get into the Holy Habit of **Prayer** for themselves and others.

If you have a closed and private group on social media for your group, invite members to post prayer requests so that other members of the group can see them and pray for them. This will encourage the group to pray for each other throughout the week, beyond just the times when they meet.

ACTS 👨‍👩‍👧

Organise a variety of events to pray in different ways, covering adoration, confession, thanksgiving and supplication. Part of these events could be teaching on different ways of praying.

Younger people may enjoy using a prayer cube or prayer hand. On each finger of the hand or face of the cube, write one of the points below and encourage people to use that to help focus their prayers:

- Adoration: tell God something you think is amazing about him
- Confession: if you have messed up, tell God; ask him to forgive you and to help you to do better in the future
- Thanks: say thank you for something good that has happened
- Supplication: pray for other people who are ill or having a hard time, or ask God to help you when life is difficult or stressful.

As the hand has a thumb too, ask people to decide what they would like to put on it – this could be a repeat of one of the statements above, or a specific prayer such as the Lord's Prayer. For the cube, there are two additional faces to add to.

Pray for your community 👨‍👩‍👧 ☺

Find out what is going on in your local community from councillors, local press, local shops or community organisations. Identify people, groups or events that need **Prayer** and set aside time regularly to do this. Take this further by putting together a prayer diary and sending text, email, or printed updates to each other.

Go on a prayer walk: a more intentional activity which can be done alone or in a group. Walks can be arranged around the house, the church or the community. You could focus on places of work, shops or 'problem areas'. Walk slowly, reflecting and listening. You could stop at key places to pray using a written liturgy or open prayers. Simon Bailey's book *Stations: Places for pilgrims to pray* (Canterbury Press, 2014) may be helpful.

If you do a prayer walk with children or young people, ask them to think about places that are important to them and find them on a map. Use a compass to find the north, south, east and west sides of the church building, then walk around the outside of the building, stopping to face each compass direction. The prayers could then be focused on those people and places that are in that direction.

Pray across 'boundaries'

Pray for all the local churches, or have a prayer time together with ecumenical partners specifically to pray for each other's churches and the local community.

Pray with your community

What events or occasions do people in your community consider important or significant, and how might these be an opportunity to share with them in **Prayer** either inside or outside the church? Days such as Remembrance Sunday, or significant anniversaries of wartime events, can be a chance to make space available for **Prayer** or to lead communities in **Prayer**.

You could also create opportunities for your community to come together to pray for specific things – many churches hold events remembering those who have died and praying for their friends and families. For something more off the wall, the House for all Sinners and Saints in Denver holds an annual Blessing of the Bicycles to celebrate being conscious of our transportation choices and the impact they have on the world.

Think about how and when the church building could be opened for **Prayer**. This can be in response to a community concern such as tragic deaths, or for commemorations and other special days, or just a regular practice.

Could you be creative and have a prayer space within your church that users of the building can access? For example, you could have a prayer tree in the main entrance where people can write their prayer on a leaf and hang it on the tree. Or you may like to design and decorate a specific room for **Prayer**. If this is to be an intergenerational space, then collect ideas for how this could be designed from children, young people and adults. It might include ideas such as:

- prayer stations
- activity space for creating, drawing and painting
- artwork or icons to help people reflect
- headphones to listen to music
- soft furnishings and lighting to make it comfortable.

You don't need to default to inviting people into your church building to pray; you can offer and lead **Prayer** anywhere that you have an invitation – hospitals, local councils, schools, coffee shops or on the streets! It is also possible to create prayer spaces where the community can join in, for example tying ribbons to railings in the centre of a town in memory of loved ones.

Occasionally (quarterly, annually)

Retreat

Take days out to pray, perhaps focusing on world issues or using the prayer resources of different charities.

Go on an annual prayer retreat. You could attend a retreat organised by others (there are a number of organisations offering retreats; see **www.retreats.org.uk** for some examples). Or you could organise something yourself, where you get away from the ordinary to have time to spend in **Prayer** and reflection. You could go on a retreat as a small group, youth group, family or individual.

Hold a prayer weekend for your church – either at your church or at a retreat centre.

Fast ☺

Fasting is a biblical principle that can be a powerful way to connect with God.

If you are planning to fast, take into account appropriate and sensible precautions for those of different ages or those with medical conditions (please seek advice from a medical professional).

Could you fast individually or together as a small group or youth group, and use it as a prayerful tool to connect with God? Could you fast for one meal, or for a whole day? Could you make it a habit to do this once or twice a year? You may find it helpful to use a journal while you are fasting.

QUESTIONS TO CONSIDER AS A CHURCH

These questions will help your church to consider how it can review the place of **Prayer** in all of its life together. They are intended to be asked regularly rather than considered once and then forgotten. You will need to determine where in your church the responsibility for each question lies – with the whole church in a general meeting, or with the church leadership, a relevant committee or another grouping. Feel free to add more of your own.

- Is there a dedicated place for **Prayer** within your premises? If so, how is this place used and how regularly is it refreshed?
- How does your church provide opportunities for members of the local community to pray? How and where do you pray for the community and in the community?
- Do you have regular meetings for **Prayer**? If so, do these need renewing in any way?
- Is **Prayer** always included in church meetings and, if so, is it done as a formality or is it considered an integral part of the meeting? Could more time be taken to pray in meetings and might **Prayer** be led in more varied and creative ways? If so, would some training be helpful?
- Who prays intentionally for the church and its activities? Do you want to form a prayer group/team to do this?
- How are prayer needs shared? Do you have a prayer chain, for example?
- How are people of all ages involved in **Prayer**? How might the children be encouraged to take a lead in **Prayer**, for example?
- What proportion of the church budget is allocated to support the prayer life of the church?

CONNECTING THE HABITS

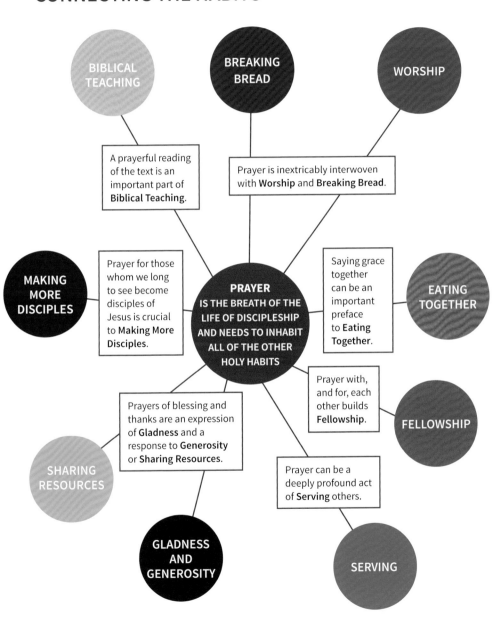

BIBLICAL TEACHING

BREAKING BREAD

WORSHIP

A prayerful reading of the text is an important part of **Biblical Teaching**.

Prayer is inextricably interwoven with **Worship** and **Breaking Bread**.

MAKING MORE DISCIPLES

Prayer for those whom we long to see become disciples of Jesus is crucial to **Making More Disciples**.

PRAYER IS THE BREATH OF THE LIFE OF DISCIPLESHIP AND NEEDS TO INHABIT ALL OF THE OTHER HOLY HABITS

Saying grace together can be an important preface to **Eating Together**.

EATING TOGETHER

Prayers of blessing and thanks are an expression of **Gladness** and a response to **Generosity** or **Sharing Resources**.

Prayer with, and for, each other builds **Fellowship**.

FELLOWSHIP

Prayer can be a deeply profound act of **Serving** others.

SHARING RESOURCES

GLADNESS AND GENEROSITY

SERVING

GOING FURTHER WITH THE HABIT

DEVELOPING FURTHER PRACTICES OF PRAYER

Continual prayer

The Jesus Prayer has a track record of centuries of use in Eastern Orthodox Christianity, but in recent decades it has become popular across different denominations in the West also. Its full form is: 'Lord Jesus Christ, Son of God, have mercy on me, a sinner,' but it is also used in shorter forms. It can be used to keep ourselves oriented to God while walking, or driving, or travelling on public transport, or doing physical work. The normal way to use the Jesus prayer is to repeat it constantly, not like a mantra, but intentionally, as a prayer. It is called 'the prayer of stability' because it aims to keep us on track with God through the day. Those who practise it regularly can achieve a silence of the heart even in the midst of activity.

Praying with and from scripture

It is possible to use words of scripture in the same way as the Jesus Prayer, for example the words of Peter in response to Jesus in John 6:68, 'Lord, to whom can we go? You have the words of eternal life.' In Centering Prayer, a single word like 'Abba' or 'Maranatha' is also a prayer taken from scripture. Beyond the use of words of scripture for supporting silent prayer or maintaining stability of life, the Psalms provide prayers for each element of 'ACTS' of **Prayer**. For example, try using:

- Psalm 63:1–4 for Adoration
- Psalm 51:1–4 for Confession
- Psalm 107:1–2 for Thanksgiving
- Psalm 54:1–2 for Supplication.

It is worth adding that hymns and Christian songs provide another rich source to draw on for use in **Prayer**.

Praying across 'boundaries'

For some groups, it may be appropriate to arrange an interfaith prayer walk, in which people from different faiths visit a number of places of worship to share in **Prayer** in each 'local' style.

'Ready-made' prayers

When you are praying, do not heap up empty phrases as the Gentiles do; for they think that they will be heard because of their many words.
MATTHEW 6:7

Jesus isn't saying that we shouldn't use words in **Prayer** at all. In Matthew 6:9, he goes on to say, 'Pray then in this way: Our Father...' Praying in whatever words come to us in the moment can be helpful, but words which are provided for us 'ready-made', whether in the Bible or in composed by others, can also be channels of the Spirit in our praying. And sometimes, as Romans 8:26 reminds us, we do not even know how to pray and yet the Spirit still prays through our 'wordless groans' (NIV).

Whether we use words from scripture or hymns or words written by someone else, these 'ready-made' prayers can speak to our hearts and become a medium for us to express ourselves in **Prayer**. Sometimes that can happen in an instant, but more often the riches of these words need to be accessed by being repeated thoughtfully and prayerfully so that they become our own and truly express our own **Prayer**. In a communal worship setting, the same can be true but there is a careful balance that is needed to avoid a fruitful Holy Habit of **Prayer** becoming the heaping up of empty phrases which Jesus warns against in Matthew 6:7 – something which even the Lord's Prayer itself is not immune to, as common Christian experience shows.

Having said that, prayers that are said or sung regularly can lie deep within our souls and be drawn upon at times when it is really hard to pray. Terry Waite, when held hostage in Beirut, found it was the formal prayers, learnt and repeated over many years, that sustained him during his dark days of captivity. One of the team who compiled this material found themselves singing familiar prayerful songs as they lay on the anaesthetist's table being prepared for an operation.

Praying with the stations of the cross

This is another ancient Christian practice that many people still find helpful, particularly during Lent, Passiontide and Holy Week. It involves contemplating and praying with 14 or 15 images of Jesus' journey from being condemned to death to the tomb, or his resurrection (the final image can vary).

You may wish to explore this as a way of praying. If you need help, why not visit the local Roman Catholic, Orthodox or high Anglican church, where the priest or people may be glad to introduce you to this way of praying?

Listening in prayer

One very important role of the use of silence in the presence of God is to underline the importance of listening in our praying – if we never stop talking, we might miss what God is wanting to say to us. Experienced pray-ers have a word of caution for us, though: God may well speak in an unmistakeable way at times, but we must not expect that God will immediately communicate some message to us just because we choose to sit in prayerful silence for a few minutes at a time. That may sometimes happen, but it is much more likely that, when we choose to orient our hearts and minds to God for a period each day, our spirits will be better able to act and think in accordance with God's purposes in the rest of our lives.

Praying by using gestures and images

A prayer word like 'Abba' can help us to orient ourselves towards God but, equally, a physical gesture like cupping our hands can also help direct our intention Godward without any verbal expression. Similarly, a visual image or an object – even a simple wooden cross – can be a way to help us as we pray. It is worth reflecting, though, on the difference between thinking about or meditating on an image or object, and an act of prayer which may flow from that. There is a difference between attention, as we think about something, and intention, as we turn our hearts to God. This is true whatever means we use to express our intentional orientation to God, whether by expressing it in words or in some other way.

Praying with an icon

The practice of praying with an icon comes from deep within the Christian tradition. *Icon* is the Greek word from which we get our word 'image'. Christian icons are often known as 'windows into heaven'. The idea that a piece of artwork can give us a glimpse of the eternal comes from the study of the person of Christ – which focuses on the Incarnation, on God being known in human form.

You could paint your own icon, or buy one from a Christian artist or Christian bookshop. Praying with an icon can be a helpful addition to a rhythm of **Prayer**, but it can take a little time to get used to. Start by simply gazing at the image, allowing what you see as the longings of your heart to interact with what you encounter, as you look at what the icon presents to you in a particular moment. Icons have a way of teaching the heart spiritual truths in a different way from the mind.

The Examen

Examine yourselves to see whether you are living in the faith. Test yourselves. Do you not realise that Jesus Christ is in you?

2 CORINTHIANS 13:5

In line with 2 Corinthians 13:5, many Christians find it helpful to take time each evening to review their day. God is never absent but, by the way we conduct our daily 'walk', we can bring ourselves more fully into an appreciation of God's presence or remove ourselves further from it. An evening review provides a way of learning from our day in order that we may walk more closely with God in future. Ignatian spirituality makes this a central element in the form of what is called the 'Examen'.

The Ignatian Spirituality website (**www.ignatianspirituality.com/ignatian-prayer/the-examen/how-can-i-pray**) has a page with information on the Examen and how to use it in one's devotions.

Body prayers/physical prayers

As you seek to deepen the Holy Habit of **Prayer**, why not reflect upon the part your body, as well as your soul, has to play in praying? Be biblical, be imaginative, be creative!

We believe in the God who created the physical world and looked on it and said, 'It was good' (Genesis 1). So, what does that mean for us as Christians to understand the relationship of our bodies to our spiritual lives, and particularly to our praying?

Archbishop Anthony Bloom writes, on pp. 78–79 of *Living Prayer*:

> There is nothing that befalls the soul in which the body does not take part. We receive impressions of this world, but also of the divine world partly through the body, and that body is therefore linked with the soul in the life of prayer.

In *The Screwtape Letters*, C.S. Lewis portrays a senior demon, Screwtape, writing with advice to a junior tempter. In letter 4, Screwtape tells him that human beings should be made to think that their bodily position makes no difference to their prayers, because it is easy for them to forget that whatever they do with their bodies will affect their souls.

Physical fatigue will naturally impact on our ability to pray. This should relieve us of feelings of guilt when, as a result of the burden of responsibilities, we find it difficult to concentrate in our prayers. But it also means that it is our responsibility, as far as it is possible for us, to maintain a healthy lifestyle with sufficient rest and sleep to allow us to pray as we should.

With regard to posture, if our intention is to offer prayers of adoration to God, what posture might best contribute to our worship? Lounging back with legs crossed? Or, perhaps, standing with hands lifted, or kneeling with head bowed? On the other hand, lying on our backs can be an appropriate position for **Prayer** at times, although maybe not in public worship.

There are different traditions in the worship of different denominations; for some, sitting is the normal posture for **Prayer**, for others it is standing, and for others again it is kneeling. But whatever positions we adopt for **Prayer** at different times and in different places, it is important to remember what Bloom and Lewis say about the connection between body and soul.

Apart from the potential effects of posture on our praying, physical movement can be a way of supporting or actually expressing our prayers. There is a variety of video material available on praying through movement, some good and some not so good. Search on YouTube for 'Praying with our bodies' by St Anthony's Priory in Durham, or for praying the Lord's Prayer with body prayer (see the online media section below).

Prayer labyrinths

Labyrinths developed in churches during the Middle Ages when Christians were encouraged to make a pilgrimage to Jerusalem, but the crusades made it too dangerous, so the church began to lay its own walking paths on the floors of cathedrals for pilgrims to walk in safety.

Walking a labyrinth is an act of prayer that can often result in transformation. For many of us, the ability to quiet the mind has eluded us. Our lives are too busy for us to sit quietly. This is why the labyrinth has begun to attract people's attention. It has only one path, so there are no tricks to it and no dead ends. The path winds throughout and becomes a mirror for where we are in our lives; it touches our sorrows and releases our joys. To enter a labyrinth is to walk with purpose and intentionality. It is a slowing down: an experience of being in the moment, in the act of opening up one's heart and mind by surrendering to the journey, and it is often this letting go that brings transformational peace.

There are three stages to walking:

- **Releasing (walking in)**
  Let go of the current thoughts on your mind: worries, anxieties, to-do list… This is an act of shedding thoughts and emotions. It quiets and empties the mind.

- **Receiving (the centre)**
  Be still. Sit or stand and stay there for as long as you wish. It is a place of **Prayer** – a place of listening and waiting.

- **Returning (walking out)**
  As you walk back out, reflect on any insights. How do they speak to your present situation? Walk back out, joining God at work in the world. Each time you walk the labyrinth, you become more empowered to find and do the work you feel your soul longing for.

You can find more information from Veriditas (**www.veriditas.org**) or the Labyrinth Society (**www.labyrinthsociety.org**) or search YouTube for 'Using labyrinths to help people pray' (**youtu.be/TI2hE-ynw0I**).

Prayer spaces ♀♀♀ ☺

You could create a dedicated prayer space in your church or, depending on relationships with local communities and organisations, you may be able to create a permanent or temporary prayer space in a community or public building such as a library, business, hospital or school. 24-7 Prayer's Prayer Spaces in Schools (**www. prayerspacesinschools.com**) has many ideas that could help you.

You will need to consider who the prayer space is for (e.g. just children, young people, general public) and plan the space appropriately. The prayer space could be quiet and reflective, or creative and stimulating, or contain a whole variety of styles.

You may also like to think about having a prayer space at home. Where in your home could this be and what could it look like?

Sharing your story

Encourage people to share their stories and testimonies about the power of **Prayer** to bring change in their lives.

People could share how the Holy Habit of **Prayer** has formed and transformed their lives by speaking at services or writing a short article for a church magazine. This could become a regular feature each month as a different member of the congregation shares their **Prayer** story.

Members of small groups could practise sharing their **Prayer** story with each other as a way of gaining the confidence to share with those outside the church at work, at school, at leisure and in the community.

ARTS AND MEDIA

There are many films and books containing scenes about **Prayer** which could be used as an illustration in worship. However, it is suggested that the following films and books are watched or read in their entirety and followed by a discussion to go deeper into the topic of **Prayer**.

Films

12 Years a Slave (15, 2013, 2h14m)

A very powerful film in which the practices of **Prayer** (spoken and sung) help to maintain Solomon Northrup's faith, hope and dignity in the face of the brutality of the slave trade. Based on a book of the same name.

- Can we pray or work generously for those who treat us badly? If so, how?

Bruce Almighty (12A, 2003, 1h41m)

A comedy in which the eponymous Bruce, who spends a lot of time complaining about God, is given almighty powers to teach him how difficult it is to run the world. In particular, he has to grapple with how to answer everybody's prayers.

- If you had God's powers, how would you answer **Prayer**? Would you want to say yes to everybody?

- Can all of our prayers really be answered?
- How does Bruce's experience of being God change his understanding of **Prayer**? What important questions does God ask of Bruce?
- Did this film challenge you in any way about your own **Prayer** life?

Facing the Giants (PG, 2006, 1h51m)

The story of an American high-school sports coach who turns to God in his hour of need to find that his prayers are answered in extraordinary ways.

This film comes from a particular theological perspective on the way God responds to **Prayer**, which may be troublesome for some. If you plan to use this film, make sure you have watched it in advance and are prepared to respond to the issues it may raise.

- How do you respond to the film's portrayal of **Prayer**?

Into Great Silence (U, 2005, 2h49m)

A slow and mesmerising meditation on the life of a silent monastic community, this film takes an understanding of **Prayer** to another level.

This film is something quite different, and wouldn't (for instance) be suitable for a general film night – make sure you watch it first if you intend to use it.

- The film describes a monastic community, a long way from most of our experience. What can we take from the spirituality of the monks and their way of life that can help us in our **Prayer** (and in living)?
- How important is a regular pattern of **Prayer**?

The Way (12A, 2010, 2h3min)

The story of a reluctant pilgrim finding community on the road and the importance of **Prayer** as doing something even though you are not sure what the outcome might be.

- With whom do you have a sense of community outside the church?
- How might you pray for, or with, those you meet?

Books: fiction

Are there people in your church or local community who would like to discuss some of these books at a book club? Guidance on how to form these is widely available online, and you could also ask denominational training officers for help.

☺ Ballet Shoes
Noel Streatfield (Puffin, 1972)

The story of three girls and their determination to achieve their dreams.

- In chapter 3, the girls make a vow with each other 'like at christenings'. In chapter 12, they make the vow again and end it with 'Amen'. Is this **Prayer**? If so, what it makes it **Prayer** – and if not, why not?
- In the book, the girls work hard to achieve their dreams. How are we called to be the answer to our prayers?

Chasing Francis
Ian Morgan Cron (Zondervan, 2013)

A great read to help people think about faith, discipleship, spirituality, **Prayer** – the lot, really.

- What form of pilgrimage might you undertake?

ᛏᚩᛏ Hillytown Biscuit Church at Garibaldi Hall
Ruth Whiter (Christian Education, 2009)

Read about Jake and his dad, and what Jake discovers while on a church weekend away at Garibaldi Hall.

- What does Jake's experience teach us about **Prayer**?

ᛏᚩᛏ Papa, Do You Love Me?
Barbara M. Joosse (Chronicle Books, 2005)

When a father in Africa answers his son's questions, the boy learns that his father's love for him is unconditional, big enough to absorb the pain of failure and create a safe space for the child to learn responsibility.

- How might you try to encourage others to rediscover, through prayer, the depth of God's love for them?

The Quilted Heart
Mona Hodgson (Waterbrook, 2013–14)

Like a beautiful patchwork quilt, the three novellas in *The Quilted Heart* tell stories of lives stitched together with love and God's unending grace.

- These books would be ideal for a reading group or book club. If you don't have one, why not form one with these or other books about prayer to start you off?

Books: non-fiction

Eat, Pray, Love: One woman's search for everything
Elizabeth Gilbert (new edition, Bloomsbury Publishing, 2007)

The story of one woman's search for meaning and peace, a search that involves exploring **Prayer**.

- Are you or your church in a place of searching at the moment? Might a journey of **Prayer** help?

God on Mute
Pete Greig (Kingsway, 2007)

A moving testimony to the power of **Prayer** in the depths of grief and questioning.

- Does God seem to be silent in the midst of suffering? If you or your church are in a time of suffering, could some of the thoughts and reflections in this book help?

Listening to God: Hearing his voice
Joyce Huggett (Hodder & Stoughton, 2005)

An accessible book from a popular author that helpfully explores the practices of listening in **Prayer**.

- What is the balance between speaking and listening in your **Prayer**, both individually and as a church? Does this balance need adjusting?

Multi-Sensory Prayer: Over 60 innovative ready-to-use ideas
Sue Wallace (Scripture Union, 2000)

An excellent practical introduction to using all of the senses in **Prayer**, with over 60 tried-and-tested prayer ideas.

- How could this, or a similar resource, help you to pray in different ways?

👪 Professor Bumblebrain's Bonkers Book on Prayer
Andy Robb (CWR, 2013)

Everything children wanted to know about **Prayer** and need to ask.

- How do you help children to pray?
- In what ways do their questions challenge you?

When I Pray, What Does God Do?
David Wilkinson (Monarch Books, 2015)

Explore this really practical question with a scientist and theologian.

- When you pray, how do you expect God to respond?

Who We Are is How We Pray: Matching personality and spirituality
Charles J. Keating (Twenty-third Publications, 2004)

A fascinating and helpful exploration of how our different personality types help to shape the ways in which we find it most helpful to pray.

- What forms of **Prayer** do you find helpful personally? What forms do others in your church find helpful? What does this book tell you about the differences?

Articles and online media

Body prayer

The Lord's Prayer, from Contemplative Fire (**youtu.be/sxWOfNqobNY**, or search YouTube for 'Contemplative Fire Body Prayer', 4m15s).

One of a series of prayers with accompanying physical movements that utilise the body as well as the mind and voice in **Prayer**. All of the movements are carefully introduced and easy to follow.

Morning Bell

Offers a new photograph each day with short words of wisdom to provide a focus for stillness and **Prayer** (**www.facebook.com/themorningbell**, or search Facebook for 'Morning Bell').

Pray as you go

A prayer website with a daily podcast of biblical material, **Prayer** and music to reflect upon and engage with; particularly good for reflective people (**www.pray-as-you-go.org**).

24-7 Prayer

The 24-7 Prayer movement – an international, interdenominational movement of **Prayer**, mission and justice – have a number of short videos on their website, including an animation about why people should pray (2m18s) (**www.24-7prayer.com/videos/animation**, or search 24-7 Prayer for 'Why pray?').

Good News Stories

Sutton Coldfield's Parish Nurse praying with people (**youtu.be/TUkkMJyvEG0** or search YouTube for 'Good News Stories with Nick').

Music

The following songs may help you to explore and reflect further on this habit.

40 U2

A powerful song of lament based on the psalm of the same number, which repeats the cry, 'How long?'

I Say a Little Prayer Aretha Franklin

A powerful soul ballad in which the singer expresses her love through a regular pattern of **Prayer** for the person to whom the song is addressed.

Poetry

A number of poems are presented or referenced below. Choose one to reflect on.

You may wish to consider some of the following questions:

- What does this poem say to you about **Prayer**?
- Which images do you find helpful or unhelpful?
- How is your practice of **Prayer** challenged by this poem?
- Could you write a poem to share with others the virtues of **Prayer**?

Prayer (I)

Prayer the Churches banquet, Angels age,
Gods breath in man returning to his birth,
The soul in paraphrase, heart in pilgrimage,
The Christian plummet sounding heav'n and earth;
Engine against th'Almightie, sinners towre,
Reversed thunder, Christ-side-piercing spear,
The six-daies world transposing in an houre,
A kinde of tune, which all things heare and fear;
Softnesse, and peace, and joy, and love, and blisse,
Exalted Manna, gladnesse of the best,
Heaven in ordinarie, man well drest,
The milkie way, the bird of Paradise,

Church-bels beyond the starres heard, the souls bloud,
The land of spices, something understood.

George Herbert

Psalms Redux: Poems and prayers
Carla Grosch-Miller (Canterbury Press Norwich, 2014)

Carla reworks Old Testament psalms for those seeking to refresh their vocabulary for **Prayer** and worship. She takes the powerful voices and themes from the ancient texts, in which no human experience or emotion is considered off-limits and the writers rage at God for life's incomprehensible cruelty as freely as they exult in life's blessings, and transposes them to a contemporary culture with recognisable images and metaphors. She also provides other completely new material, written for specific occasions and events in modern life.

Prayer
Carol Ann Duffy, from *Mean Time* (Picador, 2013)

On Prayer
Czeslaw Milosz, from *New and Collected Poems 1931–2001* (Ecco Press, 2003)

Prayer Flag
Ian Adams, from *Unfurling* (Canterbury Press, 2015)

St Kevin and the Blackbird
Seamus Heaney, from *The Spirit Level* (Faber and Faber, 1996)

This Is All the Life You Have
Adrian G.R. Scott, from *Arriving in Magic* (Author House, 2013)

Fool of God (Christ in the Garden)

Mark Cazalet (b. 1964): oil on paper, 1993, 18 x 18 cm.
From the Methodist Modern Art Collection, © TMCP, used with permission.
You can download this image from: www.methodist.org.uk/artcollection

Cazalet portrays Jesus praying, leaning over a rock in the garden of Gethsemane. This small oil was painted as a result of Cazalet's meditation upon Luke 22:39–44. It appears that a single brushstroke creates the posture of Christ; the colour palette is limited and the composition spare. The paper is handmade with a cockled (wrinkled) surface.

- What do you think is the significance of the shapes and colours, especially of the colour chosen to represent the flesh? What does this say about Christ's feelings?
- What else strikes you about the image?
- How does this image speak to you of **Prayer**? How does it challenge you in your prayer life?
- How would you paint yourself into this picture?

Thin place

George MacLeod, founder of the Iona Community, described Iona as a 'thin' place – where heaven and earth come very close together. Where are the thin places for you? Where might you discover such places even in the busy-ness and ordinary-ness of everyday home and working life?

Credits

In addition to the Holy Habits editorial/development team, contributions to this booklet also came from: Peter Ball, Tina Brooker, Fiona Fidgin, Ian Fosten, Dorothy Graham, Jill James, Joyce Mason, Tony McClelland, Ed McKenzie, Sarah Middleton, Tom Milton, Kathryn Price, Marjorie Roper, Annette Sampson, Andi Smith, Diane Webb, Karen Webber and Peter Woodall.

'This set of ten resources will enable churches and individuals to begin to establish "habits of faithfulness". In the United Reformed Church, we are calling this process of developing discipleship, "Walking the Way: Living the life of Jesus today" and I have no doubt that this comprehensive set of resources will enable us to do just that.'
Revd Richard Church, Deputy General Secretary (Discipleship), United Reformed Church

'Here are some varied and rich resources to help further deepen our discipleship of Christ, encouraging and enabling us to adopt the life-transforming habits that make for following Jesus.'
Revd Dr Martyn Atkins, Team Leader & Superintendent Minister, Methodist Central Hall, Westminster

'The Holy Habits resources will help you, your church, your fellowship group, to engage in a journey of discovery about what it really means to be a disciple today. I know you will be encouraged, challenged and inspired as you read and work your way through each chapter. There is lots to study together and pray about, and that can only be good as our churches today seek to bring about the kingdom of God.'
Revd Loraine Mellor, President of the Methodist Conference 2017/18

'The Holy Habits resources help weave the spiritual through everyday life. They're a great tool that just get better with use. They help us grow in our desire to follow Jesus as their concern is formation not simply information.'
Olive Fleming Drane and John Drane

'The Holy Habits resources are an insightful and comprehensive manual for living in the way of Jesus in the 21st century: an imaginative, faithful and practical gift for the church that will sustain and invigorate our life and mission in a demanding world. The Holy Habits resources are potentially transformational for a church.'
Revd Ian Adams, Mission Spirituality Adviser for Church Mission Society

'To understand the disciplines of the Christian life without practising them habitually is like owning a fine collection of soap but never having a wash. The team behind Holy Habits knows this, which is why they have produced these excellent and practical resources. Use them, and by God's grace you will grow in holiness.'
Paul Bayes, Bishop of Liverpool

'The Holy Habits resources are a rich mine of activities for all ages to help change minds, attitudes and behaviours. I love the way many different people groups are represented and celebrated, and the constant references to the complex realities of 21st-century life.'
Lucy Moore, Founder of BRF's Messy Church